D0057157

PRAISE FOR THE *QUICKBOOK*

"Emotional intelligence is a highly important skill for personal and professional success. This book is excellent and the learning included in the free online test is cutting-edge. I strongly recommend it."

~ KEN BLANCHARD,
THE BEST SELLING MANAGEMENT AUTHOR OF ALL TIME. COAUTHOR OF *THE ONE MINUTE MANAGER®*

"In my experience, emotional intelligence is a huge part of success for people at all levels in business. The *Quickbook* is a great synopsis of this important concept and is easy to enjoy on your next flight."

~ RICHARD LA CHINA,
CEO OF ITECH AND 1999 ERNST AND YOUNG ENTREPRENEUR OF THE YEAR

"The *Emotional Intelligence Quickbook* is not just for use in the corporate workplace! I found the EQ concepts easy to understand and helpful in raising my self-awareness and increasing my creative flow. The chapter on Team EQ was especially good for dealing with relationships within my band. This book rocks!"

~ JONE STEBBINS,
BASSIST FOR BREAKTHROUGH BAND, *IMPERIAL TEEN*, FEATURED ON MTV, HBO, AND IN *ROLLING STONE MAGAZINE*

PRAISE FOR THE *QUICKBOOK*

"I wish all books could be this useful! A truly fascinating read. It will undoubtedly change many lives for the better, as it has mine."

~ DR. MARC MUCHNICK,
COAUTHOR OF THE INTERNATIONAL BEST SELLER,
THE LEADERSHIP PILL

"The *Quickbook* is full of great stuff that can do a lot of good in the world. I breezed through it and couldn't resist taking the online test. It's a brilliant way to raise personal and social consciousness."

~ MARTHA LAWRENCE,
AUTHOR OF FIVE CRITICALLY ACLAIMED NOVELS
INCLUDING *ASHES OF AIRES* AND *PISCES RISING*

"An outstanding and important book. This is the go-to guide for the world of emotional intelligence."

~ SENIOR RESEARCHER,
THE CONSORTIUM FOR RESEARCH ON EMOTIONAL
INTELLIGENCE IN ORGANIZATIONS

PRAISE FOR THE *QUICKBOOK*

"Our clients tend to be very successful people. They are also very busy people. This book provides insights that provide high value without wasting time! My coaches and I have also done powerful work, aided by the Emotional Intelligence Appraisal™ that comes with the book. It is a fantastic tool for learning the skills that are critical to high job performance."

~ **MARSHALL GOLDSMITH, AUTHOR OF THE BEST SELLING** *LEADER OF THE FUTURE* **AND A PREMEIR EXECUTIVE EDUCATOR AS RANKED BY** *FORBES, THE WALL STREET JOURNAL, HARVARD BUSINESS REVIEW,* **AND** *FAST COMPANY*

"Intellect and experience are what get people into jobs, but emotional intelligence is what makes them star performers. This book is a great find, even for those working in technical positions. The scientific basis for what it teaches is refreshing. It literally changed my life at work AND at home."

~ **SCOTT HARRIS, MS, RAC, HEAD OF REGULATORY AFFAIRS, ATTENUON PHARMACEUTICALS**

PRAISE FOR THE *QUICKBOOK*

"This book takes the enormous subject of emotional intelligence and explains it simply. You will learn what it is, what it isn't, and—best of all—how you can easily learn to improve your EQ! A 'must-read book' for anyone who cares about their personal relationships and their professional career."

~ BONNIE BURN,
COAUTHOR *ASSESSMENTS FROM A TO Z*

"Great book for the busy professional who manages or aspires to manage a team. The authors' concise writing style gave me valuable advice in a short amount of time. Anyone leading a project-based team will find the section on EQ and Teams particularly helpful."

~ STEPHANIE LEE,
DIRECTOR, MOODY'S KMV FINANCE AND TECHNOLOGY

"I REALLY appreciated the 'quick' insights provided by the *Quickbook*. It's an easy read to give to course participants in order to inspire and excite them."

~ STEPHANIE SIERADZKI,
PERFORMANCE CONSULTANT, LCE

PRAISE FOR THE *QUICKBOOK*

"The *Quickbook* is the most concise, yet most useful, resource on emotional intelligence available. This book gives you exactly what you need to know in a fast and informative read."

~ BRIAN O. UNDERHILL, PH.D.,
A4SL COACHING AND CONSULTING

"The *Quickbook* gives you the facts straight up. The writing style is clear and concise and there is no filler to dilute the message."

~ JOANIE CONNELL, PH.D.,
LECTURER, UNIVERSITY OF CALIFORNIA

"I typically read fiction books exclusively, so I'm glad the *Quickbook* was recommended by a friend. It teaches an amazing concept that is easy to learn and actually use. It continues to have a huge impact on my sales, and it is no accident I landed my first million dollar account shortly after reading it."

~ RYAN MANGAN,
REGIONAL SALES, FORUM SNOWBOARDS

The
Emotional Intelligence
Quickbook

EVERYTHING YOU NEED to KNOW

Travis Bradberry, Ph.D.

Jean Greaves, Ph.D.

TALENTSMART
San Diego

TalentSmart®, Inc.
11526 Sorrento Valley Road
San Diego, CA 92121

Copyright © 2003 by TalentSmart®

All rights reserved, including the right of reproduction in whole, part, or any form.

The Emotional Intelligence Quickbook, TalentSmart, and The Emotional Intelligence Appraisal are trademarks of TalentSmart, Inc.

For information regarding special discounts on bulk quantities please contact TalentSmart Sales at 888.818.7627 or sales@talentsmart.com

Manufactured in the United States of America.

At TalentSmart we strive to use the most environmentally friendly paper stocks available. Our publications are printed on acid-free recycled stock paper. Our paper always meets or exceeds the minimum GPO and EPA requirements.

We dedicate this book to E.L. Thorndike, who had the insight nearly a century ago to tell the world there is more than IQ.

CONTENTS

A *Quick* Note From the Authors

This book exists because emotional intelligence (EQ) is a simple, yet practical, concept. EQ skills can be learned relatively quickly with impressive results. By simply focusing on building a new perspective around emotional intelligence, you can make a positive change that will impact the rest of your life.

In working with emotional intelligence, we've discovered the challenge is to make it accessible. Despite nearly a century of research, emotional intelligence has only been available to the public since the first book hit the shelves in 1995.

The "*Quickbook*" takes an important step by providing a speedy overview of emotional intelligence in an applied, how-to format. You will get a sound understanding of the latest in this burgeoning field.

Warmly,

Travis and Jean
San Diego, CA

The Emotional Intelligence *Quickbook*

1.

EQ is

E motional intelligence is your ability to recognize and understand emotions, and your skill at using this awareness to manage yourself and relationships with others.

While thought leaders in the field offer different approaches to bringing this definition to life, they all basically agree on one thing: Emotional intelligence (EQ) captures the side of life that typical "smarts" do not.

Emotional intelligence is made up of four unique skills that cover how you recognize and understand emotions, how you manage your behavior, and how you manage relationships. These skills are:

(1) Self-Awareness

(2) Self-Management

(3) Social Awareness

(4) Relationship Management

In 1995, Daniel Goleman began a series of books about these skills, and the more than 10 million copies in print demonstrate how useful and intriguing EQ is for anyone interested in learning and improvement.[1]

"Emotions have taught mankind to reason."

~ Vauvenargues

The four skills of emotional intelligence are important, because together they capture nearly everything you do that is not a function of how smart you are. Emotional intelligence is also a flexible skill that is readily learned.[2]

While it is true that some people are naturally more emotionally intelligent than others, there is ample research demonstrating that high EQ individuals can be made, even if they are not born.[3]

Regular intelligence (IQ), on the other hand, is not flexible. It is your ability to learn. Your IQ is the same at age five as it is at age 50. You don't get smarter by learning new facts or information.

EMOTIONAL INTELLIGENCE

	WHAT I SEE	WHAT I DO
PERSONAL COMPETENCE	Self-Awareness	Self-Management
SOCIAL COMPETENCE	Social Awareness	Relationship Management

The first two EQ skills focus on you:

(1) Self-Awareness: Your ability to accurately perceive your own emotions, and stay aware of them as they happen. This includes keeping on top of how you tend to respond to specific situations and people

(2) Self-Management: Your ability to use awareness of your emotions to stay flexible and positively direct your behavior. This means managing your emotional reactions to all situations and people.

The last two EQ skills focus more on you with other people:

(3) Social Awareness: Your ability to accurately pick up on emotions in other people and understand what is really going on. This often means understanding what other people are thinking and feeling even if you don't feel the same way

(4) Relationship Management: Your ability to use awareness of your own emotions and the emotions of others to manage interactions successfully. This ensures clear communication and effective handling of conflict.

"Human beings, by changing the inner attitudes of their minds, can change the outer aspects of their lives."

~ William James

It's Nothing New

Emotional intelligence first emerged during the IQ movement of the 1920s. Researchers testing intelligence realized that IQ did not capture all of a person's potential for success. "Social intelligence," as it was called, explained a person's ability to excel above and beyond IQ as it was traditionally measured.[4]

During the middle of the century, the behavioral psychology movement stifled the study of intelligence and emotion. It was considered taboo to explore this side of the human psyche.

It wasn't until the 1980s that emotional intelligence took on its current name, when a doctoral research study first coined the term.[5]

The introduction of emotional intelligence was not a significant departure from social intelligence. Instead, emotional intelligence provided a new model for social intelligence that was easier to understand and a better measure of these critical skills.

Research conducted shortly thereafter at Yale (in the early 1990s) was conclusive: Psychologists Jack Mayer and Peter Salovey confirmed that EQ is a major indicator of achievement, and explains why two people of the same intelligence could attain vastly different levels of success in their work and personal lives.[6]

People with high EQ have the ability to flourish where others flounder. EQ is the "something" that is a bit intangible in each of us. EQ gives a powerful name to how we manage behavior, navigate social complexities, and make personal decisions that achieve positive results.

In 1995 Daniel Goleman's first book hit the shelves. and *Emotional Intelligence* was featured on the cover of *Time Magazine*. It was the first time EQ surfaced in most people's vocabulary. This book is now in print in 20 countries and more than 30 languages, demonstrating how well EQ addresses a critical part of our experience as humans.

It's Based in Our Biology.

New discoveries about the brain in the last decade shed considerable light on the power of emotional intelligence. Until recently, scientists considered the brain "frozen" and unable to develop new connections by the time we reach adulthood. Now we know the brain is able to build new connections (called neural pathways) throughout our adult life.

We take in information from the world around us through our senses. This information travels throughout our body from cell to cell in the form of electric signals. If a mosquito bites you on the leg, that sensation must travel to your brain before you are aware of the pest.

Sensations enter our brain in one place at the back near the spinal chord. Complex, rational thinking happens in the opposite side of the brain. The electric signals entering the brain must travel to the front before we have our first logical thought about what we are experiencing.

This route can be problematic because signals first pass through the limbic system on the road to the front of the brain. The limbic system is where emotions are experienced.

The front of the brain cannot stop the emotion "felt" in the limbic system. Instead, the two areas communicate back and forth constantly. This process is the root of emotional intelligence.

I THINK
RATIONALLY
(way over here)

LIMBIC SYSTEM
(I feel here)

SPINAL CHORD
(enters brain here)

Our brains are wired to make us emotional creatures. We experience the emotional response to an event before it reaches the part of the brain that thinks rationally and reacts to the emotion.

EQ is affected by our ability to form and keep a well-traveled connection between the limbic system and the front of the brain. The more you think about what you are feeling—and do something productive with that feeling—the more developed this pathway becomes. The more traffic in both directions, the better.

The daily challenge of dealing effectively with emotions is an integral part of the human condition. New, productive behaviors actually form new pathways in the brain that connect emotional experiences with reason.

This means if I typically yell when I'm feeling angry, I have to learn to choose an alternative reaction. I must practice this new reaction many times before it will replace my urge to yell. High EQ individuals are those who make sure the road between the base and the front of the brain is a well-traveled one.

"What lies behind us and what lies before us are tiny matters compared to what lies within us."

~ Oliver Wendell Holmes

It's Not IQ or Personality

People often wonder whether smart people are also the ones who are emotionally intelligent. Research has found little to no connection between EQ and IQ: You simply cannot predict someone's EQ based on how smart they are.

The same holds true for personality. There is little connection between personality—the stable "style" of behaving that defines each of us—and emotional intelligence. Obviously, personality influences how EQ takes form in any person, but they do not occur together in a predictable way. You cannot guess an individual's EQ based on his or her personality, or vice versa.

The picture on the following page nicely illustrates the relationship between EQ, IQ, and personality. The overlap among the three is small and insignificant.

Some personality traits, such as extraversion, have a connection with specific EQ skills, such as Relationship Management. However, the connection between personality and overall EQ is unpredictable.

It is important to consider all three traits in the quest to understand any person. Practically and scientifically, EQ, IQ, and personality are independent of one another.[7] Of these qualities, emotional intelligence is the only one you can change to actively contribute to your success and happiness.

SIZING UP THE WHOLE PERSON

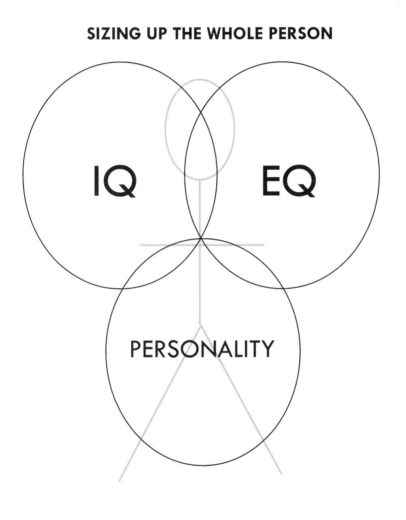

The Impact of EQ Is Measurable

What does EQ impact? The short answer is, a *lot!* The popularity of emotional intelligence during the last 15 years spawned intense scientific research demonstrating the influence of EQ on success in the workplace, physical health, and personal fulfillment.

The link between EQ and job performance is notable. Individuals higher in EQ tend to have higher performance than their low EQ counterparts. Those who work to improve their EQ—whether high or low to begin with—outperform colleagues of similar EQ levels who do not make the same effort.

Top performers in most jobs are 12 times more productive than weak performers and 127% more productive than average performers.[1] EQ accounts for more than 60% of job performance.[8]

The impact of EQ is strongest in leadership, sales, and customer service positions, where relationships are the critical commodity. Typically, 80% of high performers are also high in EQ.[9]

Organizations like American Express, L'Oreal, and the US Air Force have saved millions of dollars through EQ programs that cost just tens of thousands of dollars to implement. The case studies on the following pages are examples of model programs.

The United States Air Force in the mid-1990s was losing 35% of recruiters who could not meet quotas during the first year. To combat this difficulty, the Air Force developed a program to select recruiters based on scores on an emotional intelligence test.

After the first year of the program, only 5% of recruiters selected did not reach the quota. The 30% reduction in turnover created a $3,000,000 savings in training costs alone.

The program cost just $10,000 to implement. The results were presented in a report to Congress that generated a request to the Secretary of Defense to adopt this practice across all branches of the US Armed Forces.[10]

Hallmark Communities senior leadership high in EQ, as measured by the Emotional Intelligence Appraisal™, were 25% more productive than their low EQ counterparts. EQ was more important to executive job performance than traditional leadership competencies including integrity, strategic thinking, and focus on results. EQ coaching and team building improved group cohesion and performance for low and high EQ executives.[8]

L'Oreal interviewed potential sales leaders for EQ skills instead of traditional competencies and realized a $91,370 sales increase per head for those selected through the program. The group also had 63% less turnover than those not selected for EQ.[11]

IBM, Lucent, PepsiCo, and British Airways participated in a 500-company study that analyzed the impact of different leadership skills on job performance. Across industries, EQ was more important to job performance than any other skill and had more influence on job performance than IQ and experience *combined.*[1]

AT&T operations management (line supervisors through executives) with higher EQ, as measured by the Emotional Intelligence Appraisal™, were 20% more productive than their low EQ counterparts. At AT&T, 86% of top performers were high in EQ, while only 26% of low performers were high in EQ.[8]

The impact of emotional intelligence is also profound in our nonworking lives. Studies link EQ to personal fulfillment and overall life satisfaction, as well as resilience in the face of stress. In everyday life, higher EQ is associated with increased flexibility in the face of change and a better ability to tolerate frustration.[1]

Research presented at the American Heart Association demonstrates the positive impact of EQ on the immune system, quickening the body's recovery from disease. Cancer patients who are taught emotional coping skills and behavior management as part of their recovery program have less recurrence of cancer and lower incidence of death than those who are not taught these EQ skills.[12]

Emotional intelligence has a strong influence on health-related outcomes, because it reduces the perception of stress in response to trying situations. Emotional intelligence is linked to alleviating physical and mental conditions, such as diabetes, anxiety, and depression.[12]

Studies at the Harvard Medical School have actually mapped physical differences in the brain based on emotional intelligence. The amount of "traffic" flowing to and from the limbic system has a real impact on its size and structure.[13]

Given that EQ is a flexible skill that can be readily learned, it gives hope that we all can work toward a more fulfilling life. Any step taken to improve emotional intelligence is a leap toward realizing goals and increasing personal satisfaction.

2.

How to Measure EQ

Emotional intelligence can be measured. However, this fluid ability that describes how we recognize, understand, and manage emotions can be tricky to pin down.

It is also a challenge to climb Mount Everest, but at least your Sherpa will be willing to admit that. Allow us to address the challenges in measuring this critical skill, so you don't have to figure it out alone.

Here is how it works — When we give people a personality style test, such as the Myers Briggs Type Inventory® (MBTI), they usually feel good about the results regardless of how they turn out. Most people who do not agree with their score on such a test say, "Who can *really* measure this stuff anyway? My personality is what it is, not what this test tells me it is."

When we sit down with a client to go over his or her results from an EQ test, things are not so easy. People tend to take their results very seriously, even if they know little about the test that is trying to measure their EQ. The problem is, many EQ instruments have shortcomings that are never clearly stated to the user.

Emotional intelligence tests sell so many copies worldwide because EQ hits home and is "real" for people. EQ is a marvelous way to sum up the emotional side of life, and it is easy to understand why it's important: Human beings were made to feel.

When we share with someone how "emotionally intelligent" they are, it is often a threatening experience. Even a skeptical executive who just heard the term for the first time that morning thinks a low EQ is trouble. This is for good reason. An ample body of research worldwide demonstrates how EQ is critical to success in work and personal life.[1]

So what is the point of creating a test that tries to put a box around someone's EQ? Most of us have some idea of what we may be like in the eyes of others, but even the least self-aware among us realize that self-perception is generally tainted by how we want things to be.

EQ tests are useful because it is difficult to know exactly how we come across to other people. Each of us can benefit from an objective evaluation of our behavior.

EQ tests also give insight into trends in the population. The graph on the following page shows the relationship between average EQ scores and job title for a worldwide management sample.[2]

EQ scores increase with title until director positions and above, where they drop sharply. EQ is the single biggest indicator of success in any management position, yet scores generally decrease with title, because people are promoted for their intellect, not their EQ.

To illustrate, CEOs on average have the lowest EQ scores in the workforce. Yet, among CEOs, those with the highest EQ scores are the best performers. EQ is a better predictor of success than a CEO's intelligence or experience.

EQ AND JOB TITLE

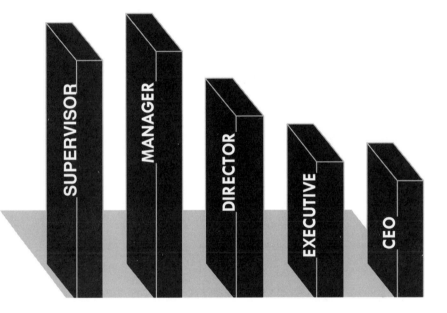

Measuring EQ also makes the learning experience more real, relevant, and personal. If I read about emotional intelligence, I may think it is a very interesting idea. I may even think hard about which of the four skills are my strengths. I'll likely remember a situation where I felt a strong emotion and was not happy with how things went.

Unfortunately, the human mind does not recall events with great accuracy. Our thoughts and even our feelings alter our perception of the experience. A well written and researched EQ test helps us learn through an objective evaluation of behavior.

The most compelling reason to measure emotional intelligence is simple. People want to know. More people look for EQ on the Internet than they do John Travolta, *The Tonight Show*, or plasma screen televisions. The Talentsmart.com website alone receives more than 100,000 unique visitors per month who are scouring the web for resources on emotional intelligence.

The intense interest in EQ spans the globe and is beginning to have a profound impact on how people work and live.[3] South Korea is an interesting example where there are public service commercials on prime-time television stressing the importance of teaching emotional intelligence to children.

"Don't bother just to be better than your contemporaries or predecessors. Try to be better than yourself."

~ William Faulkner

Choosing an EQ Test

Almost every EQ test on the market today is based on a different theory of emotional intelligence. Each theory impacts how the test works.

In truth, all major emotional intelligence theorists agree on one important thing: EQ is a person's ability to understand his or her own emotions and the emotions of others and use this understanding to manage how he or she reacts to situations and people.

The Ability-Based Tests

Authors of ability-based tests understand EQ as a naturally acquired skill or talent that people use. An ability test attempts to measure a person's ability "in the moment" as she or he performs various tasks. Tasks include rating the emotions present in pictures of people and inanimate objects, and choosing solutions to emotional problems.

Pros

Ability is a compelling theory of EQ. An ability test is generally considered to be the "purest" angle on emotional intelligence because it measures how someone responds "in the moment."

Cons

Unfortunately, ability is extremely difficult to measure. It is problematic to try to replicate the emotional complexity of the situations we encounter in the real world. As people go through an ability survey, the questions tend to seem abstract and unrelated to the stuff we have to deal with on a daily basis.

Evidence of this difficulty is found in the lack of a convincing link between these tests and job performance. Studies have measured as little as a 3% relationship between an individual's score on an ability measure and actual job performance.[4]

The Self-Report Tests

There are several self-report tests on the market and all face the challenge of getting people to accurately rate their behavior. Typically, self-report tests ask you many questions about your tendencies and have multiple options as answers for each question. Your score is based on how well your answers match patterns that indicate higher levels of emotional intelligence.

Most tests are available in a booklet with instructions that teach how to score the answers. Some tests are available online with "real time" scoring. In this way, you answer the questions and get an immediate result at the click of a button.

Self-report tests are a valid measure of EQ only when self-rating bias is adequately accounted for by the test publisher. The questions must have a method for minimizing our tendency to overrate our skills.

Good tests will have research behind them indicating reliable questions and a significant link to important outcomes in life.

Pros

These tests are cheaper, less threatening, and easier to administer than other EQ tests. They are the preferred method when the multi-rater option (covered next) is not available due to cost, or there is an inability to access others who are familiar enough with the individual's behavior to provide good feedback.

Cons

It is very difficult for anyone to rate his or her own behavior with pinpoint accuracy. Most of us overestimate ourselves, some of us underestimate ourselves, and very few of us can accurately rate our own behavior.

In selecting a self-report EQ test, it is critical that you choose one which has a system for minimizing self-rating bias.

The Emotional Intelligence Appraisal™ test that you received with this book is a good example of an assessment that greatly minimizes self-rating bias. However, if you want the most accurate measurement of your EQ, have those who know you best provide ratings via the Multi-Rater edition.

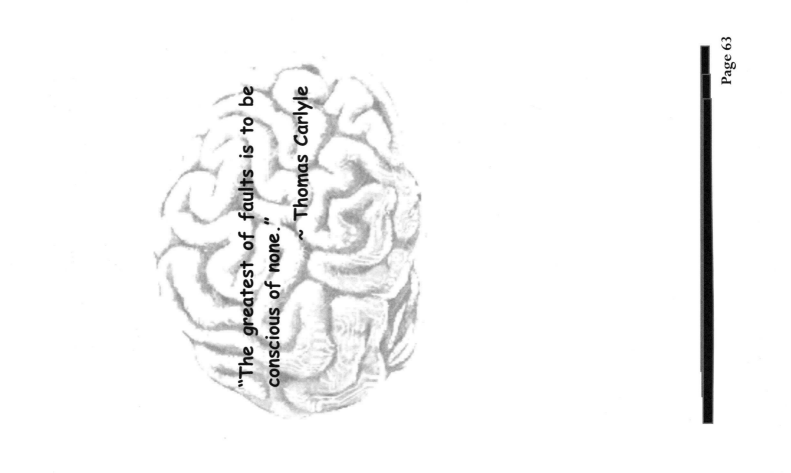

"The greatest of faults is to be conscious of none." ~ Thomas Carlyle

Multi-rater Tests

With multi-rater tests, a person invites between 3 and 12 others to respond to questions about what they see on a daily basis. The responses are summarized and delivered anonymously in a report for the person receiving the feedback to review. Good multi-rater test reports include proven strategies for improving emotional intelligence based on the individual's unique score profile.

Pros

A flood of research shows that the best measure of our EQ skill is our behavior on a daily basis. The most accurate description comes from those who work with us and others who interact regularly with us. Multi-rater test results are credible because they don't just emphasize what one person sees. Feedback comes from the group as a whole.

Multi-rater tests highlight the tendencies that others see across situations and time. These ratings tend to be largely the same, whether the person providing the rating is a peer, supervisor, or direct report. Ratings from others are more closely tied to job performance than self-ratings and deliver rich information from multiple perspectives.

Cons

There are three challenges with multi-rater tests. First, they are more costly than self-report tests. We consider this a minor challenge, given the powerful nature of the feedback and the potential for targeted development.

Second, they involve more people and more time to administer. If the test has too many questions, and one has to rate 10 coworkers for "that EQ thing," this is not fun.

Third, a person's trust can be violated if results are made public, mismanaged, or used for purposes other than the original goal of skill development.

In summary, strive for the most accurate EQ test possible in a given situation. Typically, this is a multi-rater test. However, self-assessments are still powerful. They have a strong impact on the person taking the test, even if the rating is not perfectly accurate.

It is also important to choose an EQ test that is easy to take and easy to understand. Tests that are not created with the end user in mind can make people feel like lab rats. A good test uses language that is clear and reads like a good book. Most participants will be enthralled with the process because it is a book about *them*.

3.

How to Increase EQ

Developing emotional intelligence is a long and sometimes uncertain process. But it should never be an arduous one. Improving EQ happens in the moment. Learning to pause during your day to think differently in response to your experience is all that is needed to make a significant change.

Getting to the point where you can think differently is not easy. This is the place where there is often the most discomfort. Truly improving EQ requires one to shift the focus to his or her behavior.

Whether we are higher or lower in EQ, a real change requires a new perspective and a desire to do things differently than what comes naturally.

Measure It First

Assessment is the place to start in improving EQ. We must have an accurate picture of where we are today if we are to change anything about how we manage ourselves and interact with others.

Reading and thinking about EQ are certainly effective, but making a comparison between knowledge gained and your current state is an essential part of change.

Learning becomes "real" for people when it begins where they are now, that is, at their current EQ skill level. Any good EQ learning effort should incorporate a measure of your emotional intelligence through a valid survey.

Teaching new EQ skills is important, but it is not the beginning of the development process. Skills taught must first reference our everyday behavior in an objective manner.

The results from testing current EQ levels enable future steps in the learning process to proceed successfully.

Make It Personal

As long as the EQ learner has a real measure of his or her behavior, new insights can be applied to the present situation. It is not critical how the measurement is reached, as long as it resonates with the individual absorbing the feedback.

The key to changing any behavior is to "own it" and take full responsibility for what you say and do. Taking a moment to think about your survey results is a great place to discover how you use emotions at work and in your personal life. Here, as a learner, you have the space to absorb the information, reflect on its worth, and discover what a change in emotional intelligence skills can do for you.

"The noblest question in the world is, 'What good may I do in it?'"

~ Benjamin Franklin

Take Action

The third portion of making a change is discovering what to do with your feedback. Most of us do not have the time to determine what to do next and should not have to go searching. When given action steps to follow, adult learners use life experience to make excellent use of these strategies.

The following pages contain steps you can take to increase your skill in each of the four areas of emotional intelligence.

How to Increase Self-Awareness

Self-awareness is your ability to accurately recognize your emotions as they happen and understand your general tendencies for responding to different people and situations.

Self-Awareness Action 1: Practice watching your emotions like a hawk

Before we can attend to other people, we must first learn to really understand ourselves. This means paying attention to your internal thermostat.

The thoughts and physical signs that accompany an emotionally arousing situation are the window to your internal thermostat. These are not the feelings themselves, but the beliefs and sensations that accompany them.

Everyone's thermostat reads differently, as we are all aware of different things. You might experience some of the following perfectly normal responses to emotionally arousing situations:

∴ Thoughts speed up

∴ Mind goes blank

∴ Feeling hot

∴ Feeling numb

∴ Heart beating

∴ Muscle tension

∴ Tunnel vision

∴ Tightness in the throat

∴ Tingling

∴ Trembling or shaking

"Ignoring your feelings will not make them go away. It will just help them to show up again when you least expect it."
~ Bradberry and Greaves

Self-Awareness Action 2: Track and learn your tendencies in emotionally arousing situations

Your tendencies when faced with emotion are an important part of who you are. You need to acknowledge your emotions in the moment and then take the time to think about them objectively later.

If you keep your antennae out, you will accumulate the knowledge necessary to understand your feelings in response to different people and situations.

Discover what it is about a particular person or situation that elicits your response. After emotionally stirring events, sit down and think about what happened.

Literally write down some of the things that you saw, did, thought, and felt. This will help you discover what behaviors you fall victim to when your emotions get the best of you. Talk to friends and colleagues to gain further insight. They can help you recognize your patterns and make connections that you may be missing.

The surprising thing about increasing Self-Awareness is just thinking about it will help you change, even though much of your focus will be on the things you do "wrong." Don't be afraid of your emotional mistakes. You have to know what's broken before you can fix it, and this is fundamental to heightened Self-Awareness.

How to Increase Self-Management

With increased Self-Awareness, you will be able to detect the conditions under which the second cornerstone of EQ can be built. This piece, Self-Management, is your ability to monitor your emotions so that you stay flexible and make positive choices about how you react to different situations and people.

Self-Management Action 1: Set aside time each day for problem solving

Your tendencies when faced with strong emotion are an important part of who you are. Just as preparation for a meeting leads to a better performance, preparation for a difficult situation improves your ability to manage yourself in the moment.

Self-Management Action 2: When the going gets tough, the tough pause for a moment

If you have worked on Self-Awareness, you can identify emotions that create difficulty for you and readily admit to yourself when you are feeling that way. In the moment, use this awareness to buy some time before acting.

Our thinking, our decisions, and our actions are greatly influenced by our emotions. Ignoring or minimizing feelings is a guaranteed way to let emotions control the situation. When emotions run strong, it is best to slow down and think a bit before moving forward.

Unfortunately, choosing not to run with your emotions is hardest to do when it is needed most. A tough situation is a compelling opportunity to put yourself to the test.

During tricky conversations, let the other party finish saying what she or he has to say, even if it takes a while. This will greatly decrease your chances of jumping to conclusions, and it calms the other person down.

Letting the other party finish every time he or she speaks gives you time to think. When you think before you act, you are taking the reins instead of letting your emotions lead you around.

How to Increase Social Awareness

Social Awareness is your ability to pick up on the emotional experience of others and understand their perspective. The following steps will help you build this skill, which is critical to effectively managing relationships.

Social Awareness Action 1: When you are around people, spend extra time observing, asking, and listening

Anthropologists make their living watching others in their natural state without letting their own thoughts and feelings disturb the observation. This is Social Awareness in its purest form.

You can play the anthropologist's role any time by keeping "surveillance" on your mind. You will be surprised what you notice about others when your thoughts are more on them than on yourself.

It takes practice to identify what another person is feeling, and understand how those feelings are influencing his or her behavior.

Cueing into another person correctly requires asking questions when you are not sure. To improve the accuracy of your perception, check in with others to see if you are in sync with their experience. Even when you are misinterpreting them, your attention will likely be appreciated.

Social Awareness Action 2: Learn to pick up on the mood in the room

A group of people has an emotional state, just like an individual. If you observe carefully enough in the presence of others, you will often notice a mood in the room.

Picking up on the mood in the room is similar to discovering the mood of an individual. You will see striking similarities between different people in the same group, hinting at the collective experience of emotion.

When we dive into a situation unaware of what is going on with others, our behavior is generally perceived as rude.

Groups of people sharing an experience tend to be wary of others. An activity as simple as making a presentation outside of your department at work can be disastrous if you are not socially aware.

Imagine entering a meeting after layoffs were just announced for that department. The room is filled with people uncertain about their future at the company. How would you expect them to receive your presentation?

If you do not pick up on the mood in the room, you will not ask what is going on. In this case, the state of shock and despair in the room will likely make it a long presentation for *you*.

How to Increase Relationship Management

Relationship Management requires that you apply the first three EQ skills as you relate to other people. By managing the emotions involved in an interaction, you will connect more with others and improve how people respond to you.

Relationship Management Action 1: Try to discover what role emotions are playing in your interactions with others

Understand that emotions play a part in every interaction between two people. By tuning in to emotions, you will understand and appreciate the impact they leave on otherwise benign events.

Discussions, debates, and negotiations sometimes stall for no apparent reason. Things usually fall flat when personal attachment gets in the way of resolution.

Parties will continue to disagree until emotional involvement is adequately addressed. When it is the other person who is emotional, attend to what he or she is feeling without being threatening.

In addressing the other person's feelings, you must try to be supportive, whether or not you agree with his or her actions. Being too direct in addressing the other person's feelings usually leads to defensiveness.

"The best way to become a good conversationalist is to learn how to ask good questions."

~ Mary-Ellen Drummond

Relationship Management Action 2: Use your emotions as a catalyst

There is no middle ground for emotions. They have either a positive or negative impact on every interaction between two people.

If you can ask yourself, "What do I have a knack for that helps me to get along with other people?" and use this skill, you will make great strides in forming solid relationships with others.

A good series of questions to ask yourself is:

1. Is there a way I could use this skill more often or with different people?
2. What holds me back from relating as well as I could to others?
3. Is there anything I do too much of?

No matter what your strengths are in relating to other people, there is one proven strategy that you can always use. When you have genuine interest in someone, do not hide it. Even if there are only certain things you like about someone, be sure to show it. People like people who like them.

4.

Taking EQ to Work

If you think the members of your organization are ready to discover, learn, and develop emotional intelligence skills, then it is time to explore five essential strategies for a successful EQ program.

EQ Learning Strategy 1: Begin with the individual and start at the top

Educate your senior team about emotional intelligence, what it is, and why it matters. The more they understand the business case for the skills associated with emotional intelligence, the more likely they will be interested in feedback from their colleagues on how well they apply each EQ skill on the job.

EQ Learning Strategy 2: Measure the EQ of each senior team member, followed by management and staff

This can be a self-report test if your organization cannot consider a multi-rater assessment. Self-report tests offer the least threatening method for skill discovery, though their results can be inflated by self-report bias.

Multi-rater assessments offer the most thorough and accurate assessment. Starting with an EQ test is as critical for a department- or organization-wide intervention as it is for any EQ learning you do on your own.

"If you want to succeed, you have to be smart and take a moment to think. You can't just run with your emotions."

~ Sean "Puffy" Combs

Intern turned Executive Director of Arista Records at age 19

EQ Learning Strategy 3: Provide time and help to understand feedback

There are different methods for feeding back EQ skill scores. Those that are more effective allow the person to receive the feedback in a supportive way, with discussion around the skill scores, the results for each question, and the comments.

It is easy to underestimate the time it takes to absorb the information, think about it, and talk to other people about it.

There are three methods specifically structured to help everyone hear the EQ feedback and understand it:

Feedback Method A: Group Meeting First, Then Individual Feedback

Conduct a group briefing session on the feedback stage of EQ skill development. Make the meeting brief (one hour rather than a half-day workshop). Discuss how the questions answered measure emotional intelligence skills, how to read the scores, which information to read in which order, and how to get the most out of the individual EQ feedback session.

After the group meeting, conduct confidential, one-on-one feedback meetings for each participant with a qualified feedback coach.

Each participant receives his or her EQ report during this meeting. The feedback coach talks through each section, answers questions, and guides the participant through a conversation about developing the EQ skills suggested by the results.

Feedback Method B: Group EQ Development Programs

Group development programs offer a condensed format for feedback discussions. Conduct a leadership development program around emotional intelligence, with an introduction to the concepts and model at the beginning, followed by an assessment of all participants on the first day.

With self-report EQ tests, participants can answer the questions during the session, and learn more about EQ and the four EQ skills after receiving their scores.

The leader/trainer provides general guidance on understanding the scores. Participants' scores are for their eyes only, though voluntary discussion of results in small groups can occur.

Each day of the program should focus on development strategies for each of the skills, allowing participants to observe, discuss, learn, and practice each skill. Action planning and individual confidential coaching sessions can be integrated into the last day of the development program.

Feedback Method C: Online EQ Development Programs

Online development programs provide a private, self-guided, and standardized learning process. These programs deliver access for a large number of people over a longer period than classroom training.

E-learning programs should allow for an introduction to emotional intelligence through an online assessment, as in the classroom. It is best if EQ e-learning programs tailor the curriculum to each individual's needs, based on his or her unique EQ profile.

EQ Learning Strategy 4: Give ample time for skill building, practice, and development

It may seem obvious, but skills do not develop overnight. People need at least three months to focus on one EQ skill. It takes time to practice doing new things and change old habits. Some may need work on more than one skill, so three to nine months will be necessary, with support and guidance available along the way.

"Education is not filling a bucket
but lighting a fire."
~ William Butler Yeats

EQ Learning Strategy 5: Follow up and reassess each person's EQ skills

Only after focusing significant development time on individual goals should employees measure their EQ skills a second time. This can be a multi-rater or self-report measure, but should match what was used during the first assessment.

The difference between scores on the original assessment and the follow-up assessment is the EQ change score, an important indicator of whether there has been an improvement in skill level and job performance.

5.

EQ and Teams

Just like an individual, a group of people working as an intact team have a collective emotional intelligence. Team emotional intelligence is the group's style of relating to one another, making decisions, and relating to other groups in the organization. This concept was first introduced by Vanessa Urch Druskat and Steven Wolff in the *Harvard Business Review* in 2001.[1]

Emotionally intelligent teams respond constructively in emotionally uncomfortable situations and positively influence each other.

Simply put, emotionally intelligent teams get better results and experience deeper satisfaction from working together. The basic model for team EQ is similar to that for individual EQ, though the central focus remains on the team as a collective group.[2]

Team Emotional Awareness is the team's ability to accurately perceive the emotions that influence the group. This includes accurately recognizing how each team member tends to respond to specific situations or people.

> *Example: The team's presentation to the CEO just got postponed by a month. They all feel this is a big disappointment. Members of the group sit around the table griping about all the things that won't get done according to projected deadlines.*

A team with emotional awareness skills will recognize the disappointment in the air and allow members to express their disappointment.

Team Emotional Intelligence

EMOTIONS	RELATIONSHIPS
Emotional Awareness	**Internal Relationship Management**
Emotion Management	**External Relationship Management**

Team Emotion Management is the team's ability to use awareness of the group's emotions and the emotions of team members to be flexible and positively drive behavior. This means managing the group's emotional reactions to a wide variety of situations to achieve productive outcomes that benefit the goals of the team.

Example: Using the team whose presentation to the CEO was postponed, will the group:

∴ Wallow in their disappointment by stalling all progress on the project for a month?

∴ Make the next four meetings gripe sessions?

∴ Cancel the next four meetings?

∴ Use the time to strengthen their presentation?

A team with good emotion management skills will have at least one or two members who will effectively pull the group out of the doldrums, and get everyone back on track. This does not mean telling the group to get over their disappointment, but instead to feel it, as well as begin turning to what is next.

Internal Relationship Management is the team's ability to interact effectively with each other in order for the team to respond well to difficult or challenging situations. This is the sum of the abilities of the team members to interact constructively with all other team members.

Example: One team member has been experiencing a high level of stress at home lately and is having trouble producing reports on time and without errors. The team depends on these reports for making decisions.

Does the team avoid the situation by tolerating the reports as they are? Do team members pressure the team member even more by sending curt e-mail reminders? Or is there a team member who can stop by the report producer's office to help review the draft reports? Interactions between team members outside team meetings are critical to the effective management of internal relationships.

External Relationship Management is the team's ability to interact effectively across organizational boundaries.

> *Example: A design team invites a member of the quality assurance group to their final planning session for the product design.*

Do they treat the person as an outsider to be ignored, as an extended member of their team, or as an unwelcome guest? The team that can proactively welcome the advice and concerns of the group that has the power to make a go/no-go decision is the team that uses external relationship management skills to its benefit.

Team emotional intelligence means that members of the team have and use emotional intelligence skills for the good of the group. It does not mean that all team members are emotionally intelligent all the time.

Members of the team are allowed to be human, and to have days where they feel discouraged, or even overly confident. It is important that other members of the team balance emotions that may not be realistic or helpful to the situation by helping the group remain aware.

The Impact of Team EQ Is Measurable

Though formal research on team emotional intelligence is still in its infancy, it has been clearly demonstrated that emotionally intelligent teams achieve their goals and contribute more to the success of the organization.

In 2001, Neil Ashkanasy, a researcher in Australia, published a study on the performance of teams that were low versus high in emotional intelligence. He found that teams who scored low on workgroup emotional intelligence under-performed when compared with their high EQ counterparts.[3]

Specifically, their ability to focus on tasks and achieve their goals was significantly lower than that of teams that scored high on workgroup emotional intelligence.

After weekly training in emotional intelligence skills, the EQ scores of the low EQ groups improved greatly. Their ability to focus and achieve goals reached the same levels as those of the high EQ teams.

How to Develop Team EQ Skills

Any group that wants to develop team emotional intelligence skills can. The hardest part is knowing what to work on. The following suggestions are actionable steps that any team can discuss and begin practicing immediately.

1. Take the time to get to know one another and understand each other:

∴ Together, conduct an offsite meeting to discover more about each other's values, interests, talents, and styles.

∴ Go to lunch or coffee with individual team members.

∴ Take a moment to check in with each other at the beginning of a meeting.

"Whatever we have accomplished has been because other people have helped us."

~ Walt Disney

2. Uncomfortable interactions happen for a reason. Discover the reasons:

∴ If one team member is uncomfortable, resisting, or reacting, acknowledge his or her discomfort and tell this person the team wants to understand. Find out what the reason is by asking questions and listening.

∴ When the group is uncomfortable, recognize the mood in the room and ask, *"Why is this so hard for us to discuss?"* Usually, the group will be relieved and a more constructive discussion will follow.

3. Enhance the team's emotional perspective by better understanding the bigger picture:

∴ If team members have opposing views, consider the views from each member's perspective.

∴ If everyone agrees ask, "*What are we overlooking? What angle haven't we heard or thought through?*"

∴ Ask quiet members what they think. Ask members who talk a lot to explain the opposing opinion's merits.

∴ Ask other departments/teams how they think your team is doing.

4. Discover the group's patterns of behavior that are not so productive:

As a group discuss, *"When emotions are getting the best of us, do we:*

∴ *Make decisions we regret?*

∴ *Interrupt people?*

∴ *Change the subject?*

∴ *Argue?*

∴ *Criticize each other?"*

It Is Not Always Easy

Here are some strategies to consider for overcoming the behaviors in your group that are not so productive.

When things are uncertain:

1. Someone should reinforce the team's confidence in its ability to succeed

2. Together, focus on what the group can control

3. Remind each other of the overarching goal

4. Remember how the team responded to a similar difficult situation before

5. Change the meeting times and/or increase the length or frequency, depending on what will best serve the group.

When you tend to miss out on important opportunities:

1. Don't get so caught up in your team's successes that other teams or groups resent you and resist you

2. Don't convince yourselves of your own solutions so much that you are surprised when others in the company don't share your enthusiasm

3. Don't pitch your requests based only on the needs of your team. Ideas won't take if you forget to frame them around the issues that matter to the organization at large

4. Don't sit back and point fingers if you are not getting what you need to succeed. Take matters into your team's hands, even if that means doing some of the work another team should have done.

Follow these steps closely and your team will overcome the feeling of powerlessness that groups with low team EQ experience.

EQ
Resources

Websites With Great EQ Information

www.talentsmart.com

EQ tests, books, PowerPoint®, and *BRAINS!,* the emotional intelligence training video. Emotional intelligence classroom training program and certification, as well as free EQ resources including articles and e-learning activities.

www.eiconsortium.org

A not-for-profit organization that is dedicated to the promotion and study of emotional intelligence in the workplace.

www.eisource.com

Informational website on emotional intelligence, covering workplace issues, education, and an EQ questions forum.

References

CHAPTER 1

1   Goleman, D. (1995). *Emotional intelligence: Why it can matter more than IQ.* Bantam, New York.

    Goleman, D. (1998). *Working with emotional intelligence.* Bantam, New York.

    Goleman, D., Boyatzis, R., & McKee, A. (2002). *Primal leadership: Realizing the power of emotional intelligence.* Harvard Business School Press, Boston, MA.

2   Bradberry, T., & Greaves, J. (2003). The Emotional Intelligence Appraisal: There is more than IQ. TalentSmart Publishing, San Diego, CA.

3   Ashkanasy, N. M. (2001). The case for emotional intelligence in workgroups. Symposium presentation at the annual conference of the Society for Industrial and Organizational Psychology, April, San Diego, CA.

    Clark, Callister, & Wallace. (2002). Undergraduate management skills courses and student's emotional intelligence. Manuscript submitted for publication.

    Sala, F. (2001). Do programs designed to increase emotional intelligence at work, work? www.eiconsortium.org .

    Young, D. P., & Dixon, N. M. (1996). Helping leaders take effective action: A program evaluation. Center for Creative Leadership, Greensboro, NC.

4   Thorndike, E .L. (1920). Intelligence and its uses. *Harper's Magazine,* 140, 227-335.

References

CHAPTER 1 (continued)

5   Payne, W. L. (1985). A study of emotion: Developing emotional intelligence: Self integration; relating to fear, pain and desire (theory, structure of reality, problem-solving, contraction/expansion, tuning in/coming out/letting go). Unpublished doctoral thesis, The Union Inst., Cincinnati, OH.

6   Mayer, J. D., DiPaolo, M. T., & Salovey, P. (1990). Perceiving affective content in ambiguous visual stimuli: A component of emotional intelligence. *Journal of Personality Assessment, 54,* 772-781.

    Mayer, J. D., & Salovey, P. (1993). The intelligence of emotional intelligence. *Intelligence, 17*(4), 433-442.

    Mayer, J. D., & Stevens, A. (1994). An emerging understanding of the reflective (meta) experience of mood. *Journal of Research in Personality, 28,* 351-373.

7   Burckle, M. (2000). ECI and MBTI. Hay/McBer research report.

    Graves, M. L. (2000). Emotional intelligence, general intelligence, and personality: Assessing the construct validity of an emotional intelligence test using structural equation modeling. Doctoral dissertation, CA School of Professional Psychology.

    Murensky, C. L. (2000). The relationship between emotional intelligence, personality, critical thinking ability, and organizational leadership performance at upper levels of management. Dissertation, George Mason University.

    Van Rooy, D. L, & Viswesvaran, C. (In Press). Emotional intelligence: A meta-analytic investigation of predictive validity and nomological net. *Journal of Vocational Behavior.*

References

CHAPTER 1 (continued)

8   Bradberry, T., & Greaves, J. (2003). The Emotional Intelligence Appraisal: Technical Manual. www.talentsmart.com.

9   Cherniss, C. (2002). The business case for emotional intelligence. www.eiconsortium.org.

10 GAO report titled, "Military Recruiting: The Department of Defense Could Improve Its Recruiter Selection and Incentive Systems," submitted to Congress January 30, 1998.

11 Spencer, L. M., Jr. , & Spencer, S. (1993). Competence at work: Models for superior performance. John Wiley and Sons, New York.

12 Bishop et al. (2002, Nov.). AHA Scientific Sessions, Chicago. Archives of General Psychiatry. (1993). 50:681-689

13 van der Kolk, B.A. (1994). The body keeps the score: Memory and the emerging psychobiology of post traumatic stress. *Harvard Review of Psychiatry, 1,* 253-265.

    van der Kolk, B.A., Pelcovitz, D., Roth, S., Mandel, F.S., McFarlane, A., & Herman, J.L. (1996). Dissociation, somatization, and affect dysregulation: the complexity of adaptation of trauma. *American Journal of Psychiatry, 153(Suppl),* 83-93.

References
CHAPTER 2

1   Ashkanasy, N. M. (2001). The case for emotional intelligence in workgroups. Symposium presentation at the annual conference of the Society for Industrial and Organizational Psychology, April, San Diego, CA.

Mayer, J. D., & Salovey, P. (1993). The intelligence of emotional intelligence. *Intelligence, 17*(4), 433-442.

Mayer, J. D., & Stevens, A. (1994). An emerging understanding of the reflective (meta) experience of mood. *Journal of Research in Personality, 28,* 351-373.

2   Bradberry, T., & Greaves, J. (2003). The Emotional Intelligence Appraisal: Technical Manual. www.talentsmart.com

3   Chang, J. (2003). Born to sell. *Sales and Marketing Management,* July.

CHAPTER 5

1   Urch Druskat, V., & Wolff, S.B. (2001). Building the emotional intelligence of groups. *Harvard Business Review.*

2   Greaves, J. (2003). Get emotional—it'll do your team good. *Telewest Business Outlook,* November.

3   Ashkanasy, N. M. (2001). The case for emotional intelligence in workgroups. Symposium presentation at the annual conference of the Society for Industrial and Organizational Psychology, April, San Diego, CA.

EQ PRODUCTS AND SERVICES

TalentSmart is the leader in emotional intelligence tests, training, and consulting. We offer an array of services, including free articles and resources on emotional intelligence. A brief overview of our offering follows, with detailed information available at:

TalentSmart™

DEVELOP TALENT · PROFIT SMART

www.talentsmart.com

888.818.SMART

(TOLL FREE)

Emotional Intelligence Keynotes

Have one of the authors deliver a dynamic presentation in your organization that will introduce emotional intelligence and inspire change and commitment.

Emotional Intelligence Training

Take part in the most dynamic and engaging emotional intelligence training program available. TalentSmart trainers teach EQ through assessment, interactive exercises, and blockbuster Hollywood movies in a blended solution with bottom-line impact.

EQ Training Certification

Get certified to own the Talentsmart EQ training program. Certification sessions run regularly across the country. Visit **www.talentsmart.com/eqcert** for the latest schedule of upcoming session dates.

Emotional Intelligence Appraisal™

A quick and valid assessment of EQ using Daniel Goleman's benchmark model. Measures individual or team EQ. Available online with 6 months of e-learning included, or in a self-scoring booklet format.

BRAINS!

Emotional Intelligence Training Video

No more boring training videos! *BRAINS!* brings EQ to life for your group using Hollywood movies, television, and historical events instead of fabricated clips of people "at work." Video includes Leader Guide, PowerPoint® presentation, and participant materials.

Emotional Intelligence PowerPoint®

A complete 23-slide presentation that introduces emotional intelligence and covers the latest research including the bottom-line impact in business. Best of all, the presentation plays Hollywood movies, television, and historical events right from your slides to illustrate major points.

EQ Behavioral Interviewing Guide™

80% of successful hires have one thing in common—high EQ. Walks hiring managers and HR staff through interviewing and choosing candidates high in emotional intelligence.

Share it with others...

To order individual copies of the book:

Call TalentSmart sales at 888.818.7627 ext 120

Or visit our website at www.TalentSmart.com

TalentSmart offers special quantity discounts for bulk purchases, sales promotions, fund-raising, and educational use.